# THE BRUISE OF KNOWING :

Poems: a Short History of John Monash

First published in 2019
Published by Puncher and Wattmann
PO Box 441
Glebe NSW 2037
http://www.puncherandwattmann.com
puncherandwattmann@bigpond.com

A catalogue record for this book is available from the National Library Australia.

Cover design by
Text design by Christine Bruderlin
Printed by Lightning Source International

Australian Government

Australia Council for the Arts

This project has been assisted by the Australian Government through the Australia Council, its arts funding and advisory body.

# The Bruise of Knowing

Poems: a Short History of John Monash

Phyllis Perlstone

PUNCHER & WATTMANN

*For Olive Perlstone*
*1897–1986*

# Contents

# Acknowledgements

*Previously published:*
"John Monash in Gallipoli and France": *Newcastle Poetry Prize Anthology* 2016
"The Slip": *Australian Poetry Anthology v6 2018*

*Sources:*
The many and diverse diaries of John Monash
*War Letters To Vic*, John Monash
*Australian Victories in France*, John Monash

*Biographies:*
*Monash the Soldier who shaped Australia*, Grantlee Kieza
*Monash The Outsider who Won a War*, Roland Perry
*Maestro John Monash*, Tim Fisher

Thanks to Pam Morris, Win Weir, Anna Kerdjik Nicholson, Judy Beveridge, Isabel Karpin, David Ellison, and Max Deutscher for their support, and their discriminating and helpful comments.

# PREFACE:
## Absence

The blueness and its white sheen, brighter than light on a silver
    monument
the surface of the sea is flickering on points –

yet where the sun concludes the eye's invention of difference,
constancy, that monotony of light and water working together
is a context that's the best
of absence

All night
*my* grandfather had talked, at *his* reunion with his mother
(at sixteen he'd "jumped on a ship to Australia")
when in England again
in 'The Great War
a soldier this time and caught AWOL –
this he told his daughter

Yet death had torn that daughter, small, from her own mother

To others, to me, his daughter told the story again
hushing her voice – or was it wryly pronounced
as if she understood

Turning in a usual light
her small meaning

# PART 1

# Two Incidents as Engineer / Not to Plan for them was the Mould of Disaster

*1901*
To photograph the middle span, to get it
Monash stands close –
a testing site
it's the new project
King's Bridge at Bendigo

To measure the bend in it –
skewed over the river
to suit the orders for the bridge –
Monash and Richardson, Bendigo's city engineer
decide
despite thin streaking across it
it's safe to continue testing –
a roller and traction engine
are run along to meet together
– 25 tons  at the centre –

the bridge twists
concrete bits break off
the water's splash, the crashing pieces
the slow time of gravity's next
is like glass
in an accident

the traction engine tips
and falls
on Albert Bolt, 37 years old;
pinned under it
"one arm

and one leg
severed
he's disembowelled"

Monash tries to speak
to a reporter
near him
his face muddied
shock splits into
his 'greatest regret'
'the loss of life' –
stilted, his mind's stall
words remove him from the moment –
as if he could speak for the pall
of ends in the air, of being stopped
of waiting

Monash reads out the list
to roll-call all of them
the men
in the wreck
and the shattering going on

*1898*
Monash and Vic pose for a photo
Vic's full skirt, jacket and jaunty hat
free-stand on her, almost
and match the double-breasted suit
constricting Monash
They're under the arch
of the Fyansford Bridge
just built across the Moorabool

Some workmen stand
some sit on logs –
Monash aged 33 leans one leg against a log
the workmen's limbs are half easy, too
though their jackets and trousers are looser
rumpled round their thinner figures –
their faces

intent
and nonchalant
half disowning the work
like artists sceptical of praise
they celebrate
the bridge's success

Reinforced concrete –
the invention of Monier
a French gardener
who didn't want his tubs to fall apart –
Monash saw

could 'mould
any form of beauty'

and Monash put every worker
in the picture
a corollary
for field  and groups of men
thereafter
not to plan for them was the mould of disaster

# /   In the new Barangaroo Reserve

I study the Monash photos

We walk to our favourite tree,
the same sea smell
though the wind is cooler
the same grasses between rocks
their blowing-back embroidered
pod-seed stems
peacock the air
like fans
John Monash
on long bushland hikes
wondered, as he walked –
about opportunities
improvements
in Melbourne and roundabout

As in Sydney now, walking in the city
that some dreamed we would
wish for,
the heights and bridges built –
though sometimes we want to descend from these
intersecting frets
strutting steel,
sharp-cut graze of concrete
blocking
the intimacy of trees,
dark and sun on leaves
gullies, shadows
or low leaning boughs

to bend under
stretch to see –
views undulant layering

We want sometimes the unpredictable
the gait-changing
of rock and earth
to swivel-switch our steps
twisting along a shore's
un-linear curl.
And trees –
see flickering noisy miners
hear magpies warble
setting up their branch –
we want to watch
sea gulls
whitening the blue
sitting on waves
like tiny lighthouses          /

# Monash's Turmoil

His love with Vic
no idea to soothe with easiness of his own

His work, where success needed more
than ideas or industry
and, knowing where he wasn't wanted –

Monash for respite
would climb Mount Buffalo

There where the boulders standing insecure
crevasses between them
their teetering
on fasteners strung stone to stone
to hold them
some already fallen
heaped yet smooth
beside the brush of bush and trees
and the waters canoed on by others
dressed for sight-seeing –
Monash's thoughts
could cruise
as he scaled uncertainty
in this place –
pre-history's pace
to move less in the present

no change
no achievement from his efforts was needed
except to work his feet to fit

the green and rockiness
where he ranged

# / Barangaroo

In this place that's retrieved today
from industry
at Barangaroo
this recreation of a ruined shore
buoys now sway
again, against the white trailed water
of a ferry's wake

A slipping sailing boat
and slow pleasure craft
are passing in procession too
like formal memorial-day marchers

I can think that people grouped
in 1914
like the clusters of cells on flowing streams
in the minutiae
of their bodies

Separately their only random
times of peace
within and without
couldn't last   /

# Monash was in Retreat

from hurt
before he married
Victoria Moss
His sister Mat didn't like her
Loans he'd given Max Roth
his Aunt Ulrike's husband
were hard to retrieve –
money he needed  for the life ahead

He then sees Vic
walk through the city with another man
he "attacks her behaviour"
says he's "willing to call off the wedding"
she agrees
then he begs her
"Help me to be a man
help me to be great and win fame and fortune"

# Xmas 1890

Monash hiking then
on a nine-day trip
from Beechworth
climbing Mt Buffalo
remembered
a younger self
the creeks and trees around his house
in Jerilderie

free wandering also schooled
later he wondered about Ned Kelly and his men

Once, Kelly had come
to trade horses
with his father
Louis

# / "The Slip"

With pack horses the police
in blue coats
and silver topped helmets
in sun-setting light
climb a dark height
It's precipitous

In Sidney Nolan's painting
a horse is falling
head and neck
in echoing air
drawing an oblique
a camber in the sky

one leg bent
the other arcs
the mis-step –

all aligning
breaks –

like stakes
pulled out of the ground
like palings lifting
their pointed wood
between grass
and sky
at dusk

The legs delay your glance
their slenderness
the head holds skywards
a cast of itself
fear-stiffened,

poised,
to draw towards
the curving back

The horse
in its fall
is ahead of that.     /

# Monash: *gets his degree in engineering one week before the 5th of January in 1891 when he marries Victoria Moss in the Freemason's Hall in Melbourne*

Monash is still doubtful about Vic.
He's only just given up Annie Gabriel
her softness, her love, they'd tried to elope
her husband catching him,
punching him, dragging Annie away.
The blow is like a push into his sleeping thoughts
his ambition, then, still there, he wants to keep it uppermost
to make a marriage that will steady
him, his plans to 'do' something.

Both Vic and Monash
sitting at a piano together
playing duets touch a score
each understands.
The passages hold them tense,
the sounding out of different tones stir words, worlds
heightening, merging
into a space for them together    playing
Better than speaking to their strangeness to each other.

They see Sarah Bernhardt three times
join concert groups
and go to Nellie Melba's operas

Monash, now finds Vic to be someone like himself
her eyes convince him of      he can't really tell.
Yet he wants to tell her what to do,
expects she'll respect
his 'authority'.

He's avoided Vida Goldstein, feminist,
18 years old.
Monash announces she is "all too self-possessed and affected".

Must he look for naivety then?

He soon wants to quash the quickness
in Vic. She's impulsive.
It disturbs
his studiousness

Quarrels start
He should be
"the master"
their future should be shaped
so he can succeed.

Perhaps he could now force his will
on Vic, as Annie's husband had
on Annie.

He flouted strictures as a student
wanted his freedom
dropped commitments as if he'd forgotten them.

But no breaking conventions now
they have to hold.

He has to keep himself to tasks.
He's rebuffed, frustrated by others wanting to ignore him.
He has to work harder.

So he must ignore
Vic's silences
her barbs seem petty
She complains of the way he looks
what he is wearing;

Though Monash reads George Eliot,
it's not to intuit
from a conflict, to a conclusion.
Just  a literary work
in the end.

# Vic is Physically Frail

three months after they marry
her doctor diagnoses
suspected tuberculosis;
she convalesces with her sister Belle
at Beechworth
the town that for Monash
was a stepping stone to  bushland
and Mount Buffalo

Beechworth an old gold-mining town –
Wills' expeditionary partner
Burke, was once stationed there
as Senior Inspector of Police

A prison also
had held Ned Kelly
it was where Kelly
fought a boxing match
with Isaiah "Wild" Wright

The Law and its outlaws
mixed in Beechworth,
the settling of powers, frontier ready,  –
revolving on rules
like two armies on their borders –
one indigent indifferent
to what lay ahead.
Poor equipment
like Kelly's makeshift headgear –
dark imprisoning iron –

more than masking
armour – Nolan's later icon.
He painted Kelly's followers
to look like Dickens'
'undeserving poor'
empty of proper reach.

Yet Law's endowed back-up
its establishment of powers,
like the land itself, in taken hands.
Its members rich with wealth of hills
running green or mined
with lodes of opaque grey
or black and shining.

Beechworth excludes Chinese
goldminers sent to live on the outskirts –
as in Russia
that set a place
'beyond the pale' for Jews
outside Russia's
'holy ground'

A railway line ran through Beechworth –
that Monash would travel on
past Woolshed Creek –
here the sun flashed
in blue strokes
on yellow over rocks
that stepped out of water

to great grey Eucalypts
that leaning, their leaves flowed
like slower streams
in play with the air
or stayed  like clouds in the sky's quiet –

unlike the town's
tidier trees
flanking the fine
State Bank
and set subsidiary to
its Georgian red brick
its  framed symmetries
the line of its windows –

trees as brackets
as parentheses
to hold a heritage
like flags in multiple rows
that might announce high orders

# Vic

coming back home
restored by Beechworth
has new friends
made when she'd been able, easily,
to choose and be a centre for herself

she brings a flurry around
events, around
Monash
in his unrelenting work

he's suspicious of her 'gadding about'
maybe 'running after men'

Yet when he missed out on a better job
it feels like his inadequacy
a need to make up to Vic, to promise her
things will improve

Then he's promoted at the Harbour Trust

They quarrel anyway
the differences
of present pleasures or a future
that Monash wants to achieve
to prove himself –
and it's in things Vic can't share

She's too far behind
to want to catch up, to be schooled.

Yet the feminist Vida was too forward-rushing
for Monash
who believes in his ambition, the one *he* is to achieve.
Parents and teachers used to think of his
attaining high and 'actual' power

Could he console the difference (something that might be proper)
between himself and Vic.
The strangeness he found,
her lack of opinion on things.
At a play, "The Doll's House"
he turns around, thinks she'll comment when he asks her.
She's silent
He's read in his usual newspaper, and approves of
a feminist rebuttal
of attacks on female equality

He makes efforts to 'improve' Vic
Gives her books to read.

Unconfident, Vic rejects
Monash 'improving' her
It's a condescension,
she feels       she'd have to listen not understanding
and without a clever response.

It would make obvious her lack of education.
Vic is not like Monash's sister Mat
who *was* educated.       (but without expectations)
Vic, brought up by her siblings

wants to leave things open, she thinks –
perhaps they only wanted her to be free
to see for herself

Vic , explaining to Monash,
runs from reading what he advises
it would go against her first feeling equal
with him;
the beginning of things, their same love –
music and drama

Says she's best
to 'observe'
her world –
her senses
she imagines
need no tutor

## / Damp Window in the Rain

umbrellas  passing under the fig tree leaves
hold the patterns like a slide-show
each walker giving way to another
on the wet black pavement
the tented colours screening shapes
traced like under-lit shadows
without the sun

Abstrusely a sight I turn to
reflecting on Vic
watching the hesitant configurations.
It was her time of not wanting a life rushed through
Hardly one to seize  /

# 1892    Monash is Abused and Insulted

by Lieutenant Colonel Dean Pitt
He can't get promoted to Captain
he 'thinks now'
it's 'because he is a Jew'

He's recognised by the Colonel as
having qualities
but this seems to be a fault
a reason for keeping him back
the strange dislike
sinks Monash's mood

Now he's between desire and what he will do

he twists in the spin
of what goes around him
yet keeps him out
no way to redress not being with those
he'd thought he needed
only his worth, to be among

Home from this
to quarrel with Vic
like this

his rage
distorts what they both can't stand
to stand by –
Vic can't
listen

she leaves
to be with her sister Sa
and  husband
Max Simonson

Max manages to talk to
to calm Monash

and Vic returns two days later

She conceives


He needs to monitor her
on January 1, 1893,  Monash writes in his diary
how 'proud' he is of Vic
and he imagines then a 'steadier future'
when Bertha is born
on January 22nd

# April, 30th 1893
## The Great Boom Crashes

White stars – flannel flowers – on the lid
with centre posy, ruby red waratah –
it's John William Lewin's painting
on the Strathalan Box
carried by the Macquaries in 1819
to the Blue Mountains
now repainted 1890 –
Australians
want to know themselves –
in this swell
of a forward-rushing time

Yet three years later in Victoria,
with a million people,
the great wave falls over
People in their small or large businesses
are under it,
pulling to float or escape

As in the round painted daubs of Hokusai's rowers,
faces, blank, fixed, to keep hanging on –
the rising, dark-streaked heaviness,
impending –
all are fighting its engulfing them

Monash holds on also,
finds extra,
small, chances

Then the banks are suspended

Max Roth, uncle
of Monash and husband of his Aunt Ulrike
dies in debt
Monash is executor of this will
the sons must find support for their sisters
as Monash remembers he'd had to.

Monash remembers too, his friend
Jim Lewis
who'd put in a word for him
when he was desperate
gotten him a job, his first

Monash returns a favour
finds Jim work

# Early Days

*"Words perform for inner eye we o'erlook at pleasure's peril"*

Charles Bernstein

Monash was then 20 years old –
his mother dying slowly –
his father fragile, can't support
anyone –
his mother aware and in pain
asks him to be 'responsible'
for the others

Jim Lewis, in turn, talks to Higgins
that he should take on Monash in a new project
the Prince's Bridge –

Higgins gives Monash a job –
the complete drawings
for the masonry
John Grainger, out from England
now in Victoria with his wife
and small son Percy
is the architect

A small world where
talent and desire are noticed
it isn't strange to make fine things

to press for what could be done –
friends put forward like a chorus
of eyes in focus, on whose skills fit
The Bridge,

to cross the wrinkling Yarra
in measured repetition
chords of arches
Each one's 'inner eye' to play
on these
and the river flowing.

Yet the work is enormous
for Monash
just 30 shillings a week –
less than ditch-digging earns

# Monash in 'the Crash'

resourceful now,
for 40 pounds
appeared as the expert
engineer-witness
in a libel case –
rushing his studies in Law –
Farlow, another friend from youth–
lending him 10 pounds
for exam fees –

a cost on each step –
in case learning's seen as cheap
enough for anyone
narrow doors, instead, to keep things tight, in Law,
for money only

# Ambitions

Monash's military ambition
began in the mid 1880's
in the surge of nationalism

he joined the civilian force
of the University Company D
of the Victorian Artillery

while he was bringing out
The University Review
and had aspirations to write

Later, working to support Vic
and their baby and aunt and sisters
he still enjoyed the military

he wanted to be the leader of new things
in engineering – and on to the new
weapons of war.

At the opening
of the annual gunnery course

excited to speak on what transported him
he transfixes his audience
with the intricacies
lighting his own thinking

over what was marvellous.

'Worn and nervous' next day
to sit exams

still he passes these
for Bachelor of Arts and Bachelor of Law

he can't pay the fee to graduate
for another 2 years

Vic ambitious too
in the 'lesser' world of women's fashion –
wanting to be a social success –

loves style
resembles Monash
who aspired when younger –
dressing in uniform especially –
to look good

Vic is mentioned in the Argus News
for her "ivory silk Melbourne Cup gown
with lace insertions"

this is the paper that praises
Monash
for his "first-rate style"
the lecture he presented.

He is easy, spontaneous, "note free"
on improved structure
in cannons.

# An Early Photo of Monash and Vic

looking unhappy
he's 25 and she's 21   both dark eyed
looking in separate directions
they have the same

upholding of themselves for the camera
To be seen, yet   between them
their expressions dilate with defiance,
expose opposite wishes


Monash not yet overweight
an orchid on his lapel
good-looking in a light-coloured suit
his head and neck easy in shirt and jacket
eyes and mouth in their insistence,
bright,
against the softness of his clothes

And what is inner with Vic is there
by her mouth
her dark hair and dark dress
the high collar around her neck
and head, prevent
any premature
list
or lean into
Monash's plans

not to be seen
to let unhappiness
be her helplessness

# Monash often

through his military
connections
went to Government house
without Vic
then came back, drunk

Vic
excluded
starts going out to dinner
with other men
and her sister Belle
Monash is suspicious again


Vic rages at his censure —
many times being lectured at
for her "butterfly-life"

If she had wings could she so easily alight
somewhere
for her failures –
could she wheel
in mid flight
keep buoyant
in the new weather –
young and a mother
be whom he wanted –
for his ambition
She has to ignore what she thought to be
best in her life

to think only of a future
of power and wealth
that he can gain


1894

after 3 years of marriage
taking their baby with her
Vic leaves Monash
saying she will never return

# Parting

Vic having fled from him,
Monash has to visit her,

to see his child, Bertha
at first just to hold her

and then it is a decision
he'll keep her– 'his right in law'

This he justifies
as if there's no injustice in it

Monash, then, while Vic has turned inside the house,
runs with the baby

to his father    co-opted    sitting in the car
to abduct

to keep the child
for himself

# For Vic

now having to go to Monash to see Bertha,

the loss – only to be a visitor to her child,
takes away all reason to stay

where she feels powerless
Monash's sister Mat usurps the mothering

Vic thinks, despairs – Bertha is happy without her –
and leaves the country

to travel with her brother and his wife to England
When Vic comes back,

it is for the "absence she felt of Monash" after all,
and he writes this in his diary

# PART 2

# 1910

John Monash
is photographed in London –
a prosperous traveller
a stiff white dinner shirt
rigid evening dress determines
the black and white brightness
of before
yet his eyes release
newly he's pleased
the camera records a moment –
the lines of his mouth
the success he's aimed for –
not relaxed though – and overweight
he poses a question beside his wife,
holds to hoping
that pleasure's there
for her

the conventions he's encased
around himself
After the letters between them he cannot
belie the thought,
he has hurt her self-worth

Victoria
who's slighter;
the line from forehead to throat
the lens on the tilt of her head, holds
a gaze quietened

if still 'observing' her world.
Now the forewarned weakness
of health
obscures any desire to act outside a frame
to find how she could        hover in a modernity
a life of the senses  –
                    fly her own thoughts.


            (Vida Goldstein
                    soon will print her Manifesto against war)



Bertha their daughter
leans in – in what the photographer
has caught of the family abroad,
she's pleased,
and unconstrained
by otherness to her parents
by their disharmony



Monash four years later will write a letter
to Vic

# 1914   A Letter

*"After great pain, a formal feeling comes"*
Emily Dickinson


The "honour and achievement, if he were to come back
or if he were not, would mean an honorable (sic) end"


The letter the copperplate care
of his pen on paper
before sailing to Greece
explains
how Monash saw going to war

after their idling idylls of before –


He imagines his end
in the certainty
men will be killed
and states, he has
"few years of vigour left" –


He wants
this chance to be honoured –
ambition can be
instilled within
what he was 'best, happiest at'
guiding men to a goal –
the structures they need to work together

Then
not to connect –
his small speech
to his brain's voluminous talk
that is hidden as he holds down
makes tight what he won't say –
can't –

a formal feeling comes


he writes
'regret'
that, dying he will bring her grief


it is overt
he sees war is destruction too

# Another Letter    Lemnos

*"there burst into view*
*the summit of a mighty mountain, tipped with sparkling gold*
*...the sunlight bathed its snow-clad peaks. It is Olympus...    "*

Monash gazes
at "a vast collection of ship(s)"
Lemnos harbour, as he writes, from his deck


Greece brings him
its bright flashes of Odysseus' world –
the after-image of lines  shining

in the sea in front of him
affinities with ancient minds
trail their reach to him


His costless reverie
is not like the addition
his mind begins later

to count
the fires on Lemnos at night
the dense expanse  –

how to organise
to shape the immensity
of such a universe

of questions
What is needed
in this

starry mass
of red points
in the many-tented dark


spreading
threats
of the heat of war?

# Next Day

*The "Beautiful Sea and Mild Fragrant Air"*


Monash wonders
why fight the "Turks and not
the Germans" and adds
as if to cover mis-readings
of his letter
he's "sure of the Anzacs' courage"
over the beach


when they're against the Turks –
"who're brave as well" –
it is the honour of it all


And then he watches from the ship
the first mis-step
men going uphill
into machine guns
and running  on
into cannons
continuously
firing

# Monash Landed on Gallipoli

Now aged 49 in a photo, in Gallipoli, at his headquarters, seated on a
    wooden plank
the genius of  Monash's stare is to scan, horizons assailable to thought,
    close-up


Major Paddy McGlinn beside him               a consultant officer
    opposite –
Monash, a mound of purpose
eyes still large, his head big, to the set of listening
under a tent
with flaps and roof with perching bricks      precarious as birds
uneasy to fly to plan                       of others

# "Ordered"

Monash was to "seize the High Ridge
'Baby 700'
he objects . . .
his men were exhausted"

Walker of 1st Brigade dissented too
But Godley who is "charming but selfish", Monash knows,
"with a violent temper"
and "hated by all New Zealanders"
orders it to go ahead
at night, on May 1st

2000 are killed –
When already there are 7000
casualties

Monash tells Charles Bean –
Australia's official war historian –
it is "a disaster" –
(thinks Bean will utter his concern for the soldiers)

Bean uses this report to slur
Monash    as if this shows what is breakable in him
a glassy figurehead easily "shattered"

And flawed by birth –
the son
of Jewish German parents


The once engineering tyro
His experience of losing someone under him
building the Kings Bridge had killed a man

now Monash has to look at and bear
not speak of what he had forewarned –
the thousands dead

# On Gallipoli, Dug-in

photographed
under full sun
men at the front
trousers cut to 'shorts'
improvise 'telescopes'
Monash admires their "dash"
their cleverness


they look as if it's all just
interesting work
bare legs standing
arms propping cylinders above a trench
heads in brimmed hats                 down
away from snipers

# Later

soldiers returning from rest on Lemnos
to Gallipoli in winter          hats pulled
only eyes showing          one mocking, smiles;
one, the darkness around his eyes like tears
stained-in
stares towards the camera
in a sort of soft-lipped knowing
as if to a source of witness          indifferent to his no-escape;


Within the mass of others this soldier turns
looks at the viewer; others are side-on,
are contained in an obliqueness to things
as if
deliberately not focusing –
and officers standing at the edge of the barge
peaked-capped heads pointing
towards the white-flecked sea
the illusion is they steer themselves
are in control

# /.    Barangaroo reserve


Sea swell and high shooting spray
are the first things I notice, then the breeze
and the ring around the tree I'm sitting under –
all these rocks about it
shelter feelings  –
yet the sea pulling beneath us
earth's flowing cloth


dragging its press of boats
puts me in a long moment of riding
what I've come upon – photos
and  writings of the past
except that leaves of grass and trees are soft incendiaries
on the slowness
that dissipates the bruise of knowing


it's like my friend R B's gesture
her 'thumbs down' into the earth
that makes us smile
as if we'd forgotten
our ground.

# Seagull Sounds and Sights

we're in affinity —
their nearness
almost compensates —
yet here as in any outlook
of gazing
we contemporaries enjoy
a restless sea


watch its contrast to the all about that's usual
birds flying and landing on trees
with their sounds of arrival —
even in the city, with aeroplanes and grass-mowers
and the churning, that construction workers work
out of

I'm wondering now
why Monash wanted the honours of an army chief      /

# Again Monash Writes to Vic

*I'm afraid Australia will get a terrible shock when it gets the full*
*later lists…I have been one of the few lucky ones … although men*
*have  been killed and wounded around me*

War Letters

It's a lull
everything is reflected
through an aftermath's
slow admissions
of *that which has happened*

Monash had said, without money, he had to choose his business
not a military life                                  looking good in
    uniform
the colours                                    the planned, band-led
    ceremonies
watching a drill's rhythms

The choreography
the little dance of the slow march

the present arms
reverse arms
lower
rest arms

the outstretched arm and hand
as if searching –
the ballet in perfect
synchrony

stills the eye
even as it fails
is not the unmeasured flight –
of the dazzle of dance

in the arching
and languid
steps
of eros


Whatever the stage for writing about his choice to Vic in 1898
it was
"…the social opportunities" (of the army)
…how it grieves me"
(to give these up )


If it was also a love of reaching
goals, puzzling strategies,
in war it was to be hard
to hold back his own intense
forethought
dropping it as if he could believe in
compliance,
in the arrangements of others
under their command

# Monash at Gallipoli Writing to Vic

tells of the shock Australians will get
when the number killed
is updated
yet he falls into a hope
that the vast count
meant an end to it
that the Turks
had "done their dash";


Yet to Vic then, deeper in his frankness
knowing she might need him
to explain
or even to give himself an account
of how he managed his feelings in battle –
tells her:
"one's faculties are so bound up
in the business at hand
that one simply had no time to dwell
on the horrors
or the wreckage"


yet this divulgence
must pause him
to reflect
in the time it takes
to write
to realise
what that is, "dwelling on"
what he's experienced

# Aged Fifty and after Leave

*"every day filled with horror and distress*
*the loss of precious life and the waste of human effort"*


in the society of country houses –
English nobility and French courtesy –
Monash in France
next


had to plan
the battles


After Gallipoli he needed
to invent
go past the paraded rites
the mimicking of
a plucky vicarious
gloriousness


not to be like the British officers, those who
from their classes of command
the hierarchies they followed
where carelessness
not thinking
not sparing the ranks
was forgiven
yet holding fast to equipment
valuable machines
and expending men

still couldn't stop
the Germans' hold
on sites, on towns,where infantry
were left everywhere
to bury their dead

# Getting Fit

*"A tower of strength … on the administrative side"*


Both Monash and his schooldays' friend McGlinn
(later Brigadier General)
Both, when first in Egypt, overweight,
had been Tweedledum and Tweedledee


When Monash was in charge, after, in France – challenged
to manage brigades and then divisions –
finally the whole Australian Corps of men –
Monash fitted himself to the work
surprised that "trimming down felt better, not weaker"

# Messines Ridge 7 June 1917

Monash co-ordinates
constructs ways as he means
to get one layer of large thinking over the next
through channels of cool, keep his breath on it
blow together all the streams of
where the land goes
where the men will be
when he has time to plan
to tell each where
and the time to be there –


his war is
he'll keep one relay
baton on to the second
but staying there, then starting
with piled up firing and exploding –


that is what is horrific afterwards –
to say the deaths
will be pushed into the holes his mind's
making till aftermaths
restore


to count, then, that the time's piece
is ready
that he's saving for reckoning

a war-ending he's game for


just now it's to get the soldiers
hot food by 7pm
going into the next whatever
and have the fallen picked up
for their wounds
not to leave them there

# Passschendaele Disaster

*'Haigh's Crash-Through Inhumanity'*

The only way across the mud
is on duckboards

It made the men sitting ducks

Under dry conditions the wounded falling
could be saved
In the mud they sink and drown

Those that stay on the boards
high and heads up balancing
picked off by machine guns
platoons of them dropping
into the black, thick-cake-mix earth
lumpy
with men
killed

Monash foresaw it all
had seen it
with Godley's rushed unplanned
pushes       on Gallipoli

Now Haigh impatient
blind to see another win

like Broodseinde and Messines when Monash had planned
so carefully
insists he can't wait


So Monash can only plan for ambulances
more ambulances        than ever  before


The Australian Third Division –
 3,200 casualties out of 5000
New Zealand's casualties  3,500

It is the end of Haigh's control of the Australian Army

# Showing their Hand

Murdoch and Bean take exception to
Monash's "exceptional
eclectic
intellect"

"the Jew will always get there"

How Murdoch, a journalist and Bean, the war historian
try to prevent his appointment
to be corps commander of the Australian Forces
to Monash is strange

Dealing with that prejudice
while managing all his responsibilities of command
Monash responds

it's difficult "fighting a pogrom"


Well, it will be considered
an error
Murdoch and Bean will have to eschew

# The Future

to us already
we know
more hands will show

will rise for
'that salute' for the corporal
Adolf Hitler–

who in this past
1918
is behind the lines
a dispatch-runner
far from the Front
He's not brave     can't get the Iron Cross

till  the German Army Lieutenant
Hugo Gutmann, a Jew
puts in a word for him

1937
The next future past
has Gutmann             arrested
by Hitler's Gestapo

His old regiment friends
help him escape

# Diary

*"Motor to St Gratien See Hobbs. To Bussy see Gillibrand*
*Allonville see Drake Brockman. Glissy to see*
*Brand, learnt he was not in so saw Craig (G111)"*

Monash on Wednesday July 17, 1918
writes in his diary, and daily
until the 8th of August –
the date of the battle at Amiens –
that the German Army's General Luddendorff called
a 'Black' day
one from which he would count
no possible victory thereafter


A swift running pen
a scrawl
Monash driving around noting for himself
his commanders' plans
or lack of them
in a car handed-down
from a high-starred general
who'd needed two
in case one broke down
Monash has mobility
and is a voice
to those in command
to rely on
his understanding
the totality in planning
"the immense organisation"
he'd already speculated
such vast numbers needed

In France Monash sees the same spot attacked and lost
routinely by the British and the French

Out of all ordinary practice
he worked out special  plans :
to protect his men with tanks
not to follow the troops, but moving side by side
with them, firing
with artillery
and tank-guns together

Taking planes too
to spy out where the armies were beforehand
by subterfuge

# Hamel then on to Amiens

*The "plane" flying quite low, usually at not more than 500 feet, the observer
would mark down by conventional signs on a map the actual positions of our
infantry, of enemy infantry or other facts of prime importance... The "plane" then
flew back at top speed to Corps H.Q., and the map... dropped in the middle of an
adjacent field, wrapped in a weighted streamer of many colours... then brought
by cyclists into the staff office... There can be no doubt that the whole operation
was a complete surprise both to the troops opposed to us and to the German High
Command*

*The Australian Victories in France in 1918*, John Monash


Monash is in charge then finally – in France with a whole corps –
Prime Minister Hughes listens and approves, despite himself
not to Murdoch and Bean
but to British high commanders
who need Monash's skill  –
to turn things around


The weight of battalions of tanks
robotic predators
the metal clank
of their ridged
coil-covered wheels
like caterpillars
enlarged under a microscope
in body-full tipping up
then flattening in leaps
roll into the German lines
like surprises, in the  early morning;

Monash had moved them unseen, slowly
over hard ground
on nights before
for miles

# Two more photos    August 1918

The troops of the 5th Australian Brigade
both Infantry Artillery and Tanks
waiting
for the second stage of the attack          that Ludendorff called
a 'black day"
The Australian soldiers faintly visible          in small groups          in
     sepia colour print
the camera is taking from a distance,          their standing about
amongst the sparse clumps of grass
here and there                                        on the sloping land


the lines of two ditches keep the men apart
as they wait
from the top of a ridge
and down hill
beside an almost merged shape of a tank –
it looks desultory, the men as though they're bored –
you need to guess at the apprehensions and readiness
of the soldiers
The camera tells a distance
it precludes knowing,
the image masking how they feel
Numbness of the viewer at such havoc
what is it, for the photographer, as he's halted
to see them jammed
in the landscape
far off

Then the photo
of German dead
the stillness in humps of clothes
lying beside pieces of pipe in a trench, all sorts of rubbish, rubble –
and casually falling arms, one with delicate slim hand
another cast over a forehead
and one fallen, back straight but with knees bent;
a pack of cartridges uppermost on a belt
on one in the foreground
his head down on the earth

Still photos –
capturing even minimal movement        challenges the camera
with soldiers                        waiting for battle –
yet the subject of the dead
Monash's horror after
"precious life" lost in such "waste of human effort"
speaks for his men's presence
before he saw them lifeless


we see them, fixed in their distance
as soft gestures                    on paper
yet now too
as if, inadvertently, we're walking into a room
that they've arranged themselves in      for sleep –
their deaths' immediacy
lodged shades of who they were once
deepening

# Monash

at 14 years of age had gazed large eyed
his longer-necked looking up to others
an adolescent assessing –
yet not completely settled into that –
In a photo portrait
the expression is a look of
what he sees for himself
in the world –
to tell him what to do

Later a business man –
fleshy around his head
in set-back position, worrying –
his look is
foregoneness
even when success strokes his face
with pleasure in prosperity

steadiness in his large eyes still
yet inactive stolidity
weighs back his head
immobility –
the photographer
catches a heaviness
that's not in his wife Vic
her slightness in the camera is the quietness of lost health

War's eruption in 1914
Monash gets his choice like others 'to be a man'
to win 'fame'
a piece of what is special in life.
knows he can be a leader in something
or will it be loving something
or will he be loved, admired by the people – Australia.
Monash saw war as his chance
the military is his means.

That which stultifies the time –
unshifting customs un-relinquished powers everywhere
the young held on long-lasting  leads
'white superiority'
'lesser' races pushed back
and women in their early days, only,
of suffrage –
a  new end to these stagnations is
to 'rush to arms'
to horror
and war    full-of-ends

# When as General

Monash in the field at Camon, on July 13 1918
awards  a medal to a soldier whose face in folds smiled
like Monash's too they seemed similar figures
The soldier's easiness
gives them the look of equals in independence
The award from a general to a soldier in a tin hat
looks as if they were sharing a joke against the times –
just two older men


Monash's respectful nephew and aide Siminson,
standing back, smiles shyly to see them joining hands


Another photo taken of Monash awarding a medal
is where the light is tipping the soldier's face
in the fine unfinished line of being young      the general and his aides'
noses and chins
are lit, solid forms
the boy is at attention                stiff   with what's
     momentous


Monash looks solemn               almost about to
     remonstrate
he holds the award in his hand
like the hot token it is
afraid of condoning something
around the soldier, the child in him
there in the field of war

other soldiers seated and about
don't look up
they stretch    and rest    are indifferent     heads in home matters
letters or mending


like the farmers in Breughel's painting
and Icarus falling
from a sunny sky

# PART 3

# Monash in England    then Back in Australia

Still held in by what is stark –
then it's in the dark of deaths he saw

old images, the incessant exercise
of his brain's means in war

now he's caught in the whirl of the end –
its celebrations

Monash has a tremor in his hands
a wire vibrating still

the nerves that carried signals to his actions – planned –
the neural sparks on lines, that fired from call to call

that lighting him, each message burned as it was sent –
worked, now, into his palms

shaking who he is  – who'd loved  recognition
just for his young man's looks       his presence –

yet now to enjoy a fame for these efforts
his and his men's

to reconcile fame with the lost
luminousness – of lives annulled; their numerousness


In England then, the love for Lizette, his wife's friend
since the war began – a betrayal his daughter would realise –

was his comfort
support for him; the touch between them bringing back

the melt into blood's steady beat again –
the arrest of being cold – that crystal set of accuracy,

his mind, that had kept on sending
thoughts to structure destruction

now to defend is not to allay anything –
love's lightness is –

lifting him, Monash, like Titian's Bacchus –
painted as he whirls, and turns away

from the followers he's spoiled –
to see and love, Ariadne's stilling light –

or was it her loneliness  –
Monash then, from war's addiction

could sober on the love of Lizzie
could like the wine god , struck by love's

shock, undo that for which in this time,
without  its warmth, there wasn't time enough

# His wife Vic

dares the long voyage
though sick, to rejoin Monash in England

he leaves Lizette – love, loyalty or from convention
When she's by his side, or their daughter Bertha

he's more acceptable                the buzz
is around the three-star general – twice knighted

While Billy Hughes, Australia's Prime Minister
could promote Monash to four-stars

he fears Monash will be a rival at home;
decides instead he will organize the soldiers

returning –                delay him until after elections –
upsetting Charles Bean the war historian

who sees this as ever more prestige
for the Jewish Sir John Monash

rather than Bean's Major General Brudenell White
Still, when Vic and Monash, later, land

in Australia, they meet huge crowds
Their faces in a rare sameness      Vic lets lapse

her life's hazing that she's soon to die
smiles smooth her face to joy's one form

like Monash's, rolling up war's pall of
irremediable memories

His face's happiness deeply indenting
what was blank      taut      always,

now his smile, lit vivid
as the flowers Vic's holding

# Retrospect and Consequence

Hughes in France, looking
to be known on the scene

Monash gesturing impatience for the jobs
ahead; their agitated walk, "their rush to be rid

of each other"     then it's Monash leaning towards
Hughes, needing more discourse –

hoping to persuade Hughes who
grudgingly perceives the issue  –

since it is the battlefield     These interchanges
disappear for Monash in Australia

The war over, there's no managing anything
with Hughes who has power

pulls allies around him like the stiff-faced
parochial and prejudiced

Governor General Ronald Munro who holds
a dull aloofness from the cheering crowd

to remind of his status; his mouth holds
in a line of not-being-there – in abstention

from smiling on Monash, his young daughter
Bertha and the brave-faced Vic;

as well he signals to them as will others
there'll be no place for Monash, no given rank

or position in a future to reward him
no post that a government might organise:

Monash will be hidden
removed from mention or reminder of his talents

# Monash and Recognition for the Troops

Hughes is hostile
Monash insists, begins the Anzac Day's

remembrance, rides the march
with Hobbes

War's ending not relieving the grieving
they determine to salve with a ceremony –

and the requests of soldiers or their loved ones
he'll fulfil

as he can – they're many, despite the Prime Minister
keeping him in shadows;

yet Monash's horror-shadowed thoughts
are enough

when  those who expect he'll set the country
straight, like Arthur Streeton, the artist, his friend

who want him to be a dictator, now
that the economy's failing

Monash reminds the factions
that his actions in war were for his country

This would be "to usurp Governmental power …
I have no ambition to embark on High Treason"

as he answered one in a letter that
that was what he was asking for

as many did in their new *sleep of reason*
calling for military rule to oust democracy

He knows he's best at planning and creating –
establishes The Victorian State Electricity Commission

To use brown coal he gets advice from
German experts (it is against the unreconciled)

yet it's Monash's consolation, life left
to make complex with work

something for his child's children

# 1931

Monash's last Anzac day
He rides at the head of the march, in uniform

with general's hat
Sitting on his horse standing still

his face is like patience in a portrait –
then side-on, on the move, his face a fastening effort

to pull himself forward when his determination is tired
his horse holds him as he holds his horse

The horse is grey its eyes are dark
he guides it with one arm

We can't interrogate Monash's shaded gaze
only his mouth – pulled as if by a tethering

and then the bit to his jaw
as if inhered with his troops'

changed chances for their lives
their warnings of war's consequences

like the neatness
of crowds coming out with hats on

then leaning stretching to see
It was grief's ceremony still

to strain – to reach out
to the soldiers who were alive

# AFTERWORD:
## A Short Peace

For the moment
the sea is slate blue; ferries smooth or even slow over it
we keep up our pace walking

Then we don't, they're gone
Solitary and quiet away from tall buildings
and even the thready-fine towering cranes

that crisscross steel of several
which in slow motion pass each other;
and then now, with tall trees to gaze to

and the sandstone rocks
to rest our eyes
we're in the sweet unmade freshness

where water laps away the city's dryness